SandCastle 1

Capital Letters

Months

Amanda Rondeau

ABDO
Publishing Company

Published by SandCastle™, an imprint of ABDO Publishing Company, 4940 Viking Drive, Edina, Minnesota 55435.

Printed in the United States.

Cover and interior photo credits: Corbis Images, Digital Vision, John Foxx Images, PhotoDisc, Stockbyte

Library of Congress Cataloging-in-Publication Data

Rondeau, Amanda, 1974-
    Months / Amanda Rondeau.
      p. cm. -- (Capital letters)
    Includes index.
    ISBN 1-57765-612-1
     1. English language--Capitalization--Juvenile literature. 2. Months--Juvenile literature.
  [1. Months.] I. Title. II. Series.

PE1450 .R66 2001
428.1--dc21
                                            2001033021

The SandCastle concept, content, and reading method have been reviewed and approved by a national advisory board including literacy specialists, librarians, elementary school teachers, early childhood education professionals, and parents.

Let Us Know

After reading the book, SandCastle would like you to tell us your stories about reading. What is your favorite page? Was there something hard that you needed help with? Share the ups and downs of learning to read. We want to hear from you! To get posted on the ABDO Publishing Company Web site, send us email at:

sandcastle@abdopub.com

About SandCastle™

Nonfiction books for the beginning reader

- Basic concepts of phonics are incorporated with integrated language methods of reading instruction. Most words are short, and phrases, letter sounds, and word sounds are repeated.

- Readability is determined by the number of words in each sentence, the number of characters in each word, and word lists based on curriculum frameworks.

- Full-color photography reinforces word meanings and concepts.

- "Words I Can Read" list at the end of each book teaches basic elements of grammar, helps the reader recognize the words in the text, and builds vocabulary.

- Reading levels are indicated by the number of flags on the castle.

Note: Some pages in this book contain more than five words in order to more clearly convey the concept of the book.

Look for more SandCastle books in these three reading levels:

Level 1
(one flag)

Level 2
(two flags)

Level 3
(three flags)

Grades Pre-K to K
5 or fewer words per page

Grades K to 1
5 to 10 words per page

Grades 1 to 2
10 to 15 words per page

Aa Bb Cc

Months start with capital letters.

Aa Bb Cc

The first month is January.

Aa Bb Cc

I got a balloon in February.

Aa Bb Cc

It rains in March and April.

Aa Bb Cc

I pick flowers in May.

Aa Bb Cc

Summer is in June and July.

Aa Bb Cc

School starts in
August or September.

Aa Bb Cc

Leaves fall in October and November.

_Aa Bb Cc_

What letter does
December start with?

(Capital D)

Words I Can Read

Nouns

A noun is a person, place, or thing

balloon (buh-LOON) p. 9
flowers (FLOU-urz) p. 13
leaves (LEEVZ) p. 19
letter (LET-ur) p. 21
letters (LET-urz) p. 5
month (MUHNTH) p. 7
months (MUHNTHSS) p. 5
school (SKOOL) p. 17
summer (SUHM-ur) p. 15

Proper Nouns

A proper noun is the name
of a person, place, or thing

April (AY-pruhl) p. 11
August (AW-guhst) p. 17
December (di-SEM-bur) p. 21
February (FEB-yoo-er-ee) p. 9

Verbs

A verb is an action or being word

23

The Months

January
February
March
April
May
June
July
August
September
October
November
December